I0711091

This book belongs to...

....

....

....

A
Acorn
Apple

a   animals

B
Barn
Boy

b
bee
bird

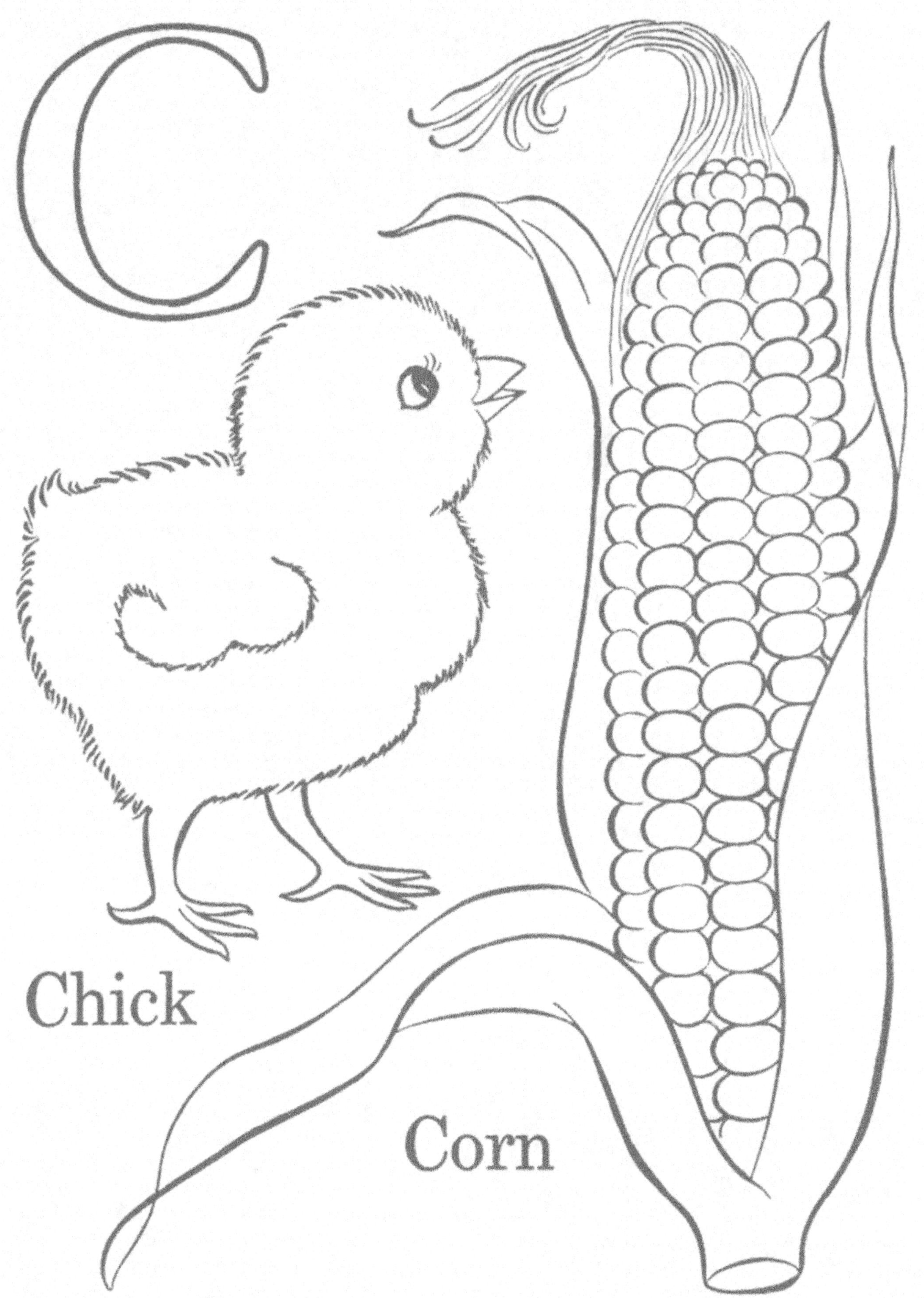
C
Chick
Corn

C
cow
carrots

D
Dog

d
duck

Eggs

F

Farmer

G
Goat
Goose

H

I

Iron

ice-skate

i

J
Jam
Jam
jug
j

K
Key
kitten
k

L
Lamb
leaf
1

M
Moon
Mouse

Nuts

Nest

O

Owl

Onions

P
Pig
Pumpkin
Puppy

Q

Quilt

R
Road
Rabbit

S
Sheep
Squirrel

T

Turkey

U

Umbrella

u

V
Vegetables
V

W
Wagon
Wheel

W

window

water
pump

X
Xylophone
X

Y
y
Yard

Z
Zipper
zinnia
Z

www.ingramcontent.com/pod-product-compliance
Lightning Source LLC
Chambersburg PA
CBHW081024260726
48662CB00026B/3079